Gratitude Journal for Kids

in 5 Minutes a Day

FUN PROMPTS AND ACTIVITIES FOR THANKS AND POSITIVITY

MELISSA KLINKER

ILLUSTRATIONS BY
ADITI KAKADE BEAUFRAND

ROCKRIDGE
PRESS

To Vivienne and Thomas, my almost-there-by-a-hair middle schoolers—you are, without a doubt, my biggest joys (even on the days when you complain about homework).

Interior and Cover Designer: Scott Petrower
Art Producer: Tom Hood
Editor: Erum Khan
Production Editor: Nora Milman
Illustrations © 2021 Aditi Kakade Beaufrand

ISBN: Print 978-1-64876-648-0
R1

TODAY, I'M THANKFUL FOR . . .

Your good friends are people you value—people who make you laugh, brighten your day, and motivate you. Who are your good friends, and why do you value them?

_____

_____

_____

_____

_____

_____

_____

_____

_____

_____

_____

_____

_____

TODAY, I'M THANKFUL FOR . . .

Nostalgia means remembering happy times you've had in the past. It's the feeling you get when you remember a toy you loved when you were little or a game you and your friends played in kindergarten. What were your favorite things when you were little? How does it feel to remember them now?

TODAY, I'M THANKFUL FOR . . .

Watering a plant makes it grow. Just like plants, when we give anything the care it needs, it grows. When you are in tune with the little things that make your family happy, you'll grow your own happiness, too. What small things can you do around the house to make each of your family members' happiness grow?

TODAY, I'M THANKFUL FOR . . .

Sometimes, spending a lot of time with your family can drive you nuts. But those little things that bother you about them—like the goofy nickname they have for you, or their humming around the house—may also actually be things that you love. What are some little things you love about each of your family members?

TODAY, I'M THANKFUL FOR . . .

Enjoying the present is important, but thinking about the future can be just as important. What are five things you are excited about for the future?

ACTIVITY

Art is a great way to express yourself. Using colored pencils, list five people in your life you are grateful for—a coach, a teacher, your parents, or anyone else. Draw each person's name in a way that represents them—use doodles, big bold letters, or a cursive font.

> # Feet, what do I need you for when I have wings to fly?

—*Frida Kahlo,
artist and activist*

TODAY, I'M THANKFUL FOR . . .

Think of yourself as a craft project. A craft project requires lots of different supplies, like paper, glue, and paint. **You** also require a lot of different supplies—like family, friends, and hobbies—to become complete. What supplies do you need to complete your "craft"? Why is each of those supplies so important?

TODAY, I'M THANKFUL FOR . . .

Part of being grateful is forgiving your own mistakes.
Write down a mistake that you made recently and why
you are going to forgive yourself for it.

TODAY, I'M THANKFUL FOR . . .

Do you focus a lot on what others are doing, at school or online, and feel like you aren't a part of it? FOMO (the fear of missing out) is real—and frustrating! Instead of basing your feelings on other people's lives, try changing your perspective and focusing on yourself. Look around you now. What do you see that makes you smile?

TODAY, I'M THANKFUL FOR . . .

Practice enjoying a really simple moment—the wind on your face, the feel of your pet's fur, or the smell of the air outside. List three really simple things you will experience joy from today, or three things you already experienced today that gave you joy.

TODAY, I'M THANKFUL FOR . . .

Spending time with people who have a positive influence on your life can feel great for both of you. Who in your extended family (an aunt, a cousin, an uncle, a grandparent) makes you feel great? What do you appreciate about spending time with them?

TODAY, I'M THANKFUL FOR . . .

When you are proud of yourself, it can make you feel more confident and more able to appreciate all the wonderful things in your life. List three things that make you proud of *you*.

TODAY, I'M THANKFUL FOR . . .

Being humble means you don't need praise for doing something good. It goes hand in hand with gratitude, because when you appreciate what you have, you see that making a difference is what really matters. List the ways that you can make a difference without needing to be praised for it. It can be something as small as putting your dishes in the dishwasher, or as big as picking up trash at your local park.

ACTIVITY

Start a family gratitude jar. Grab a large jar or can and write "Family Gratitude Jar" on it. Place a pen and a sticky- note pad next to the jar. Whenever one family member is sparked by gratitude for another family member— because of something they've done, said, or just because—have them write the person's name and why they felt grateful for them on a note. Then fold it up and place it in the jar. At the end of the week, bring the jar to the dinner table and read the notes over dinner!

> We are all more blind to what we have than what we have not.

—Audre Lorde,
writer and activist

TODAY, I'M THANKFUL FOR . . .

Volunteering your time is a surefire way to spread kindness. It could be as simple as cleaning up after an extracurricular activity ends, or offering to walk a neighbor's dog. Where could you volunteer your time to help someone you know?

TODAY, I'M THANKFUL FOR . . .

There is something magical about when the school week is finally over. What do you love most about weekends? What are you excited to do next weekend?

TODAY, I'M THANKFUL FOR . . .

Some days, it's hard to know what to do. Maybe your friends are arguing, or you saw someone break a rule at school. In situations like this, it can be difficult to know whom to listen to. List three people who have your best interests in mind—parents, relatives, coaches, or other people who care about doing the right thing. When you feel pulled in different directions, ask one of these people for advice.

TODAY, I'M THANKFUL FOR . . .

Connection can mean different things to different people. For some people, it means talking over the phone; for others, it means doing something together in person. What is your go-to way to stay connected with friends and family?

TODAY, I'M THANKFUL FOR . . .

What holiday is your absolute favorite to celebrate?
Why are you grateful for this holiday?

TODAY, I'M THANKFUL FOR . . .

Being vulnerable feels risky, even though sometimes it may be the right thing to do. Have you ever been in a situation where you were out of your comfort zone, but you chose to do something anyway because you knew it might lead to something positive?

TODAY, I'M THANKFUL FOR ...

What, or who, inspires your creativity (your artistic side), your strength (your commitment), and your determination (your hustle)?

ACTIVITY

Everyone worries sometimes. When you feel worried, you might bite your nails, tap your toe really fast, or chew on your pencil. But there's a better way (and it leaves your cuticles and pencils intact): a worry box! Grab an empty tissue box, decorate the outside, and keep it on your desk or nightstand. When you are worried about something, write it down and place it in the box. When the worry is out of your head and on the paper, you will likely worry about it less.

Nothing is impossible. The word itself says, 'I'm possible!'

—*Audrey Hepburn,*
actor and humanitarian

TODAY, I'M THANKFUL FOR . . .

Extreme joy is more than just the happiness you might feel when hanging out with your friends or eating your favorite dinner. When you feel extreme joy, you feel it deep inside you. List some things that, when you think about them or see them, you feel extreme joy.

TODAY, I'M THANKFUL FOR . . .

Happy, Sneezy, Sleepy, Grumpy, Dopey, Bashful, and Doc are the Seven Dwarfs—each named after their character traits (well, except for Doc). Which character trait do you think describes you today? Which do you think will describe you tomorrow?

TODAY, I'M THANKFUL FOR . . .

When a parent compliments you, it feels great. But you know what feels even better? Complimenting them right back. The next time a parent compliments you, bounce a compliment back to them, like a game of ping-pong. Is it possible to keep the compliment ball bouncing? For how long?

TODAY, I'M THANKFUL FOR . . .

List a few things you are worried about that haven't happened yet. By doing this, you'll free up space in your mind to focus on the present instead.

TODAY, I'M THANKFUL FOR . . .

Music is powerful. It can make you feel happy and relaxed and totally turn your mood around. What are your go-to songs that make you happy?

TODAY, I'M THANKFUL FOR . . .

Role models are people you look to as positive examples. While you may have role models of your own, you probably haven't thought about how *you* might be one to others. Imagine you have a YouTube channel with millions of followers. What would your channel be about? How could you use your platform to be a great role model to those who are younger than you?

TODAY, I'M THANKFUL FOR ...

When you give someone a compliment, it can brighten their day and give their self-esteem a quick boost. What is a compliment you received recently? Why did it make you feel grateful?

ACTIVITY

Short inspirational quotes, phrases, or words about staying focused or doing the right thing can be great motivators. Seeing these words actually written out can be even more helpful. Grab a pad of sticky notes; if you don't have them, loose paper and tape will work, too. On each note, write a positive word or simple phase—like "hope" or "you can do it." Now place these all over a space where you spend a lot of time—your room, your locker, or even the kitchen refrigerator. Seeing these simple visual cues throughout the day will make you smile, help you stay focused, and motivate you.

Forever—is composed of Nows.

—*Emily Dickinson, poet*

TODAY, I'M THANKFUL FOR . . .

....

Just like a snowflake, there is no one in this world quite like you (even if you're a twin!). List five things that make you *you*. They could be things that make you stand out in a crowd, or things that make you similar to your peers.

....

....

....

....

....

TODAY, I'M THANKFUL FOR . . .

Stress is like a rubber band. If you stretch it too far, it will snap. Stress may seem like something you can handle at first, but if you keep taking on more and more, you might snap at people you are close to, or even yourself. How do you combat stress from classes, chores, sports, and anything else?

TODAY, I'M THANKFUL FOR . . .

We have to be careful with how we use technology, but
if we use it safely, it can help us connect with people.
What are some ways that technology can help you
better connect with your parents, grandparents, or
siblings?

TODAY, I'M THANKFUL FOR . . .

When you give someone your full attention, you show them respect. One way to give someone your full attention is by disconnecting from your devices (phones, tablets, TVs, etc.). What are some ways you can challenge yourself to disconnect—for an hour, a day, or even a week?

TODAY, I'M THANKFUL FOR . . .

Mindfulness means being aware of the impact you have on your surrounding, and the impact your surroundings have on you. If that sounds confusing, try closing your eyes. Now open them and pick one object to look at in detail. Try to notice something about it you've never noticed before. What do you see?

TODAY, I'M THANKFUL FOR . . .

Gratitude comes in all shapes and sizes: You might feel grateful for big things, like clean air or a house to live in, or small things, like hearing a bird sing or spending time with a friend. List three big things you are grateful for and then three small things you are grateful for.

TODAY, I'M THANKFUL FOR . . .

Frustration can be difficult to work through. Thinking about things in a different way can make all the difference. For example, maybe something frustrating is really a chance to learn something new. What are you frustrated about this week? How can you think of things differently and turn it into something positive?

Doesn't it make you smile when you receive a letter in the mail? It's a fun surprise that's rare these days. Writing a letter, even just a simple note of "hello" or "thank you," is a wonderful way to spread kindness and make someone feel good. You don't even have to mail the letter—you can just hand it off to someone. Which people can you give a note to this week (a neighbor, the mail carrier, a librarian, a firefighter, a store clerk)?

"

Be thankful for what you have; you'll end up having more. If you concentrate on what you don't have, you will never, ever have enough.

"

—Oprah Winfrey, TV personality and entrepreneur

TODAY, I'M THANKFUL FOR . . .

Although sometimes it might not feel like it, there
is always someone who is going through something
worse than you. How can you help someone else today?
Is there a friend, a neighbor, a parent, a teacher, or a
sibling who could use your help?

TODAY, I'M THANKFUL FOR . . .

Animals can teach us to be our best selves through their loyalty and friendship. If you could be any animal for just one day, what animal would you choose? What does this animal teach you about being your best self?

TODAY, I'M THANKFUL FOR . . .

The word *beautiful* can be used to describe a person, a place, a thing, or an idea. Can you think of something beautiful you've experienced, like an amazing sunset, a concert, or a painting? What was your most beautiful experience?

TODAY, I'M THANKFUL FOR . . .

Sometimes, important people can influence us in positive ways—like a friend encouraging you to try out for the school play because you love acting. Have you ever felt like your choices were swayed for the right reasons? Why were you grateful for this? What did you learn from it?

TODAY, I'M THANKFUL FOR . . .

Being resilient means you can bounce back when things get rough. One way to quickly bounce back is finding the silver lining—the bright side of a situation. Can you think of one positive thing about a situation that you're having a hard time with?

TODAY, I'M THANKFUL FOR . . .

One way to encourage yourself is by creating an affirmation. Affirmations are sort of like pep talks you give yourself when you are feeling down. An affirmation might be something like, "I know I can do it," or "I can make that goal." What is your affirmation?

TODAY, I'M THANKFUL FOR . . .

List the top five important things in your life right now. Don't hesitate. Just quickly write whatever comes to mind. They can be people, places, things, or ideas. Go!

ACTIVITY

Anxiety about something at school, with your friends, or at home can sometimes feel really difficult to deal with. But there are some quick techniques you can use to get through these stressful moments. These three steps can help refocus your thoughts, making you feel calmer and more grounded—even in moments when you're not feeling anxious.

- Take a quick walk outside.

- Close your eyes, block every noise out, and concentrate on your breathing.

- Smell something—an unlit candle, a perfume, even soap. Yes, it's weird, but scent triggers a response in your head and will distract your brain from the anxiety that is washing over it.

We have to do with the past only as we can make it useful to the present and the future.

—*Frederick Douglass, writer and abolitionist*

TODAY, I'M THANKFUL FOR . . .

You've probably heard the phrase "laughter is the best medicine." List three things that made you laugh uncontrollably this week.

HA
HA
HA

TODAY, I'M THANKFUL FOR . . .

People and relationships are kind of like tacos. Yes, tacos. You are the shell, your family is the meat, and your friendships are all the fixings you put inside. Without all that stuff inside your taco, it's just an empty shell, right? Which people make up your taco? Who makes you feel complete?

TODAY, I'M THANKFUL FOR . . .

Doing something all on your own, without the help of a parent or teacher, can give you the ultimate sense of pride and confidence. List some things you are able to do independently, without the help of someone else.

TODAY, I'M THANKFUL FOR . . .

Sometimes, feeling calmer can make us feel more grateful, too. What are some ways you can make your bedroom or your personal space feel calmer? Could you hang a calming picture or play some soothing music?

TODAY, I'M THANKFUL FOR . . .

Though awkward or embarrassing moments might feel like they last forever, they actually don't last long. Sometimes, we even learn to laugh at the moments that once embarrassed us. What moments in your past felt truly mortifying when they happened, but seem funny now?

TODAY, I'M THANKFUL FOR . . .

What are five things you are really great at?

TODAY, I'M THANKFUL FOR . . .

Just like a storm, when anger builds inside of you, it can be fierce and powerful. What are some techniques, like breathing or counting to 10, that have helped you calm down in the past?

Yes day! Say "yes" to three things that you might normally pass on—things like playing a game with a younger sibling or helping a parent with a project. Were you surprised at how saying "yes" to these things made you feel?

For the great doesn't happen through impulse alone, and is a succession of little things that are brought together.

—*Vincent van Gogh, painter*

TODAY, I'M THANKFUL FOR . . .

Life doesn't always go as planned. But sometimes, that's not a bad thing—because it may actually turn out better than you thought it would. Can you remember a time when this happened to you?

TODAY, I'M THANKFUL FOR . . .

Talking to parents and teachers is so valuable, but sometimes you may also want to talk to someone your own age. Maybe you had an argument with your sibling, or you got really exciting news. Have you ever been grateful you had a friend to talk to? What can you do to help them in return?

TODAY, I'M THANKFUL FOR . . .

Generosity means being kind and giving more than
is actually needed. What are some ways you can
be generous and give back to your community in
extra ways?

TODAY, I'M THANKFUL FOR . . .

You can't always control your thoughts, but you can control how they make you feel. When you write down negative thoughts, you leave them on paper where they can't bother you anymore. Then it's easier to come up with something positive to replace them with. Try it: Write down a negative thought, then swap it for something positive.

TODAY, I'M THANKFUL FOR . . .

Think about a difficult part of your day. Rewrite the
story in a funny way—add characters, or change the
plot or setting. Be creative, and have a good laugh
rereading your story back in a new way.

TODAY, I'M THANKFUL FOR . . .

Smells can trigger feelings, emotions, and thoughts of a person or place in an instant. What smell reminds you of your favorite person? Your favorite place?

Date: / /

TODAY, I'M THANKFUL FOR . . .

Small and simple changes at home or school can help
the earth and make it a better place to live. You can
help through simple actions like recycling at home.
What small changes can you make in your day that will
have a positive impact on the earth?

ACTIVITY

Emojis are a fun way to communicate quickly and effectively. Draw an emoji or group of emojis for each person that you care about. Each emoji should positively describe who they are and their character qualities.

The greatest
work that
kindness does
to others is that
it makes them
kind themselves.

—*Amelia Earhart, pilot*

TODAY, I'M THANKFUL FOR . . .

Being responsible means people can depend on you. Having responsibilities means you are in charge of something. What are some things that you are responsible for in your household? Why are these good responsibilities to have?

TODAY, I'M THANKFUL FOR . . .

Imagine you are on a desert island. Whom would you like by your side until you are rescued? Is there anyone besides your parents and siblings who you'd like to be stuck with? Why would you be grateful to have them there with you?

....

....

....

....

....

....

....

....

TODAY, I'M THANKFUL FOR . . .

Enjoying ourselves can be really hard to do when we are focused on the past—the things we "should've," "would've," "could've" done. List three things from the past that still bother you. Once you've written them down, try not to think about them anymore.

TODAY, I'M THANKFUL FOR . . .

....

It's okay to not have total control over every moment
of your day. What are some things that you enjoy doing
where you don't need to control the outcome, like
reading a book or listening to music?

....

....

....

....

....

....

....

....

....

....

....

....

....

....

Date: / /

TODAY, I'M THANKFUL FOR . . .

If you're feeling down, trying to be positive and grateful can feel like one more thing to worry about. But gratitude isn't something to worry about. In fact, it's supposed to help you feel better. Write down what gratitude is to you—and the next time you're feeling down and don't know what to feel grateful for, turn back to this definition.

TODAY, I'M THANKFUL FOR . . .

Wouldn't it be nice if there were a few extra hours in the day? What would you do with those extra hours? How would they have a positive impact on you?

TODAY, I'M THANKFUL FOR . . .

The best characters in books and movies feel like real people. Who is one fictional character you'd love to swap places with for a day? Why do you admire this character?

ACTIVITY

While having a meal (dinnertime is a great time for this), go around the table and ask each person to share something from the day that they are grateful for. If they are stumped or hesitant to share, a good way to break the ice and get started is to ask everyone what made them laugh today. You'll get some tid-bits about everyone's day and laugh at some good jokes in the process!

When one door of happiness closes, another opens; but often we look so long at the closed door that we do not see the one which has opened for us.

—*Helen Keller, writer and activist*

TODAY, I'M THANKFUL FOR . . .

An entrepreneur is someone who designs and creates their own business. If you were to become an entrepreneur today, what kind of business would you have? How could you make something or offer a service that would help people?

TODAY, I'M THANKFUL FOR . . .

Movies can transport us to amazing places all around the world, or even to other worlds. If you could take a trip to any of the places you've seen in the movies, where would you go? Why would you be grateful to be there?

TODAY, I'M THANKFUL FOR . . .

Writing something nice on the sidewalk in chalk, or on a sticky note on a classmate's desk, can really brighten someone's day. List some things you'd write to encourage someone or brighten their day.

TODAY, I'M THANKFUL FOR . . .

When you aren't worried about past regrets and future worries, you notice more things. What do you notice about your surroundings right now that you are grateful for?

TODAY, I'M THANKFUL FOR . . .

School teaches us about the world around us, lets us see our friends, and helps us learn from our teachers. What are your favorite things about school?

TODAY, I'M THANKFUL FOR . . .

Courageousness means being brave and doing the right thing. Name someone you know (or maybe someone you've read about) who has shown courage. Why do you think they are courageous?

TODAY, I'M THANKFUL FOR...

If you looked your name up in the dictionary and it described you in five words, what would those five words be?

ACTIVITY

When you start your day with a smile, it really sets the tone for everything that comes after. Today, don't just start with your own smile— help someone else in your family smile, too. Anonymously make a family member's bed today, or simply do a chore without being asked. How cool is it that you had a personal hand in affecting a family member's smile in a positive way?

> It takes courage to grow up and become who you really are.

—*E.E. Cummings,*
writer and artist

Acknowledgments

I am immeasurably grateful to have such an amazing husband, who continually and unconditionally supports all of my crazy ideas; my mom, who encourages me every day with her strength and love (I love you more!); and my dad, who, although he sadly never got to see this book come to fruition, taught me about love, hard work, and compassion all throughout his life. I am also forever grateful for my sister and brother, who through thick and thin and from coast to coast will always be my biggest cheerleaders, and for my in-laws, who are constantly supportive in too many ways to mention. And last, but certainly not least, I cannot leave off my squad of wondrous girlfriends who are my family in every way, from supportive cards, to surprise gifts, to endless texts—you know who you are, and I love you all dearly.

About the Author

 **Melissa Klinker** in a nutshell, and not in any specific order, is a homeschooler, planner creator, quote lover, art teacher, graphic designer, and kindness believer. Melissa has spent a little less than a decade blogging on her kid-centered website, MamaMiss.com, and writing several articles about gratitude and service projects, which gave her plenty of ideas for writing her first book on gratitude. Melissa is also a lifelong journal writer and devourer of inspirational quotes, to the point of ridiculousness (there are 79 different quotes hung on the walls throughout her house— yes, she counted!). She always tries to look on the bright side of moments, although reluctantly sometimes, and what those moments teach her.

CPSIA information can be obtained
at www.ICGtesting.com
Printed in the USA
JSHW050829030921
18320JS00003B/3

9 781648 766480